Why Everything You Know about Robin Hood

Is Wrong

K C Murdarasi

First published in Great Britain, 2018

Published by Hephaestion Press

hephaestionpress.wordpress.com

ISBN-10: 1-916490-90-5
ISBN-13: 978-1-9164909-0-1

Dedication

For Lynne, the adopted Yorkshire lass.

By the same author:

Patrick of Ireland: The Boy Who Forgave

Augustine: The Truth Seeker

Leda

Office Life (and Death)

A New Year's Trio

Contents

1: He lived in Sherwood Forest

When I was a child, I was taken on a school trip to see the Major Oak in Sherwood Forest. The Major Oak is the biggest oak tree in Britain, propped up with so many poles that it looks like someone is trying to erect a circus tent, but we hadn't been taken to Nottinghamshire to learn about arboriculture; this tree was supposed to have been the hideout of the famous outlaw Robin Hood.

That was pretty exciting stuff for primary school children, but even then there were doubters in the class. The tree is certainly ancient – between 800 and 1,000 years, probably (you'd have to cut it down to be sure, which seems a little destructive). But the legend of Robin Hood is at least 600 years old, and probably older, so it wasn't an ancient tree when he was around. It is certainly huge, too, with a canopy that stretches 28 metres, and a trunk ten metres in circumference. But the hollow at the heart of the tree – the famous hideout – is pretty snug. You could see it providing a temporary hidey-hole for three or four people, provided they were good friends, but if we're going to believe that Robin Hood spent any serious time in this tree, possibly with his merry men, we might as well believe in the old lady who lived in the shoe as well.

Despite these obvious problems with the Major Oak as a domicile, it's easy to see how the tree could have become associated with Robin Hood. After all, it must have been in existence whenever the famous outlaw stalked the land, and it's in the heart of his base of locations, Sherwood Forest. Except that Robin was not based in Sherwood Forest. He was a Yorkshireman.

The Robin of the ballads makes no secret of the fact that he likes a bit of deer poaching in the king's forest, and Sherwood was a royal forest, where hunting deer (or pretty much anything else) was illegal. But the 'Shirewood' (so called because it covered almost the whole shire, or county) is only namechecked in one early ballad, *Robin Hood and the Monk*. The place that comes up again and again, and which seems to have been Robin's main base, according to the ballads, is Barnsdale.

And it's not just the ballads, which admittedly can easily be adjusted to appeal to local interests. Robin Hood is mentioned by a few fifteenth-century Scottish chroniclers, too. One has Robin operating in Barnsdale; another placed Robin in Inglewood (near Carlisle) and Barnsdale; and the third said that 'Robyn Hode, with his accomplices, infested shirwode and other law-abiding areas of England with continuous robberies'. Based on this, it's reasonable to assume that Robin spent some time in Sherwood, but Barnsdale is a much more likely candidate for the place he called home.

So where is Barnsdale? There are two main candidates. One is in Rutland, a tiny little county in the East Midlands of England, to the south of Nottinghamshire. The other is an area between Pontefract and Doncaster, in deepest Yorkshire. The Rutland Barnsdale was a game park, which looks promising for a known poacher, but there are two major problems with it. The first is that is wasn't called Barnsdale in medieval times – it was still called Bernard's Hill at that point. The other is that Barnsdale is mentioned in the ballads in connection with things that are very close to the Yorkshire one, not the Rutland one. Robin, standing in 'Bernesdale', tells his companions to

> 'walke up to the Saylis,
> And so to Watlinge Strete'

in order to find an impromptu guest for dinner.

Watling Street was a local name for the part of the Great North Road that ran between Worksop and Ferrybridge – passing through Barnsdale – and it really was infested with outlaws in the late Middle Ages; people who had to pass through it were well-advised to take an armed guard. The Saylis was a nearby plantation overlooking the road, a good lookout point. Yorkshire's Wentbridge is also mentioned in a ballad (*Robin Hood and the Potter*). It is, as you might expect, the site of a bridge – a bridge carrying the Great North Road over the river Went, in Barnsdale.

Barnsdale wasn't actually a forest in the technical sense of the word (land set apart for the king to hunt – no poaching!), but presumably it contained enough cover to make it worth a highway robber's time to hang around there. There are certainly a good number of trees there now. In any case, it's a lot easier to pop over to Watling Street before dinner if you're coming from the Yorkshire Barnsdale rather than the Rutland one, 80 miles to the south.

Robin wasn't confined to Barnsdale, of course. A few other locations are mentioned in the earliest references to Robin Hood. Nottingham features a lot, mainly in the form of the Sheriff of Nottingham, but Robin also visits Nottingham to go to church, for example.

Inglewood is a puzzler, as it is so far away from Yorkshire. There's not much to go on from just one reference, so it's probably impossible to tell if it was a mistake (perhaps because a similar outlaw gang operates there in the ballad *Adam Bell*), or there was another Inglewood that was nearer, or Robin Hood just got about a bit more than you would think.

And then there's Sherwood, which Robin would have had to pass through to get to Nottingham anyway, and which he probably relieved of the odd deer, but he didn't set up home in a tree there. Of course, as an outlaw, it would make sense to move around more than the average law-abiding citizen, which might explain why the Robin of the ballads seems to think nothing of dropping in on Nottingham, 50 miles from Barnsdale (although there is another theory about his Nottingham connection – see chapter four). But even if his travels took him in and out of Nottinghamshire fairly regularly, the place he came home to was Barnsdale, in Yorkshire.

2: He was of noble birth

Robin Hood was originally Robin of Loxley, a nobleman cruelly stripped of his inheritance when he fell into disfavour with the king (or Prince John), and that's what drove him to live in the woods as an outlaw, right? In modern versions of the story with happy endings, Robin even gets his inheritance back when the king forgives him. But Robin didn't have any inheritance to lose. He was what was known as a yeoman.

'Yeoman' originally meant young man, but by the fourteenth century it had come to mean a type of social standing rather than an age. It referred to a rank between peasant and nobleman. Yeomen were freeholders who cultivated their own plot of land – comparatively well off, but certainly not aristocratic. The early ballads of Robin Hood make it quite clear he was a yeoman – *Robin Hood and the Potter* makes a big deal of it, since it is addressed to other yeomen as its target audience. So how did the idea arise that Robin was a disinherited nobleman?

The first person to make it up – sorry, to find a mysterious 'olde and aunciente pamphlet' showing that Robin Hood was actually a disinherited earl – was the Tudor historian Richard Grafton in the 1560s. He never did produce his sources. Anthony Munday, a Tudor playwright, expanded on this theme a few decades later, writing plays in which Robin was Robert, Earl of Huntington, an outlaw in the forest during the time of King Richard the Lionheart. Evil Prince John also takes to the woods in the play, and tries to seduce the lovely Maid Marion.

So does the idea of Robin being Earl of Huntington hold water? On the plus side, there were Earls of Huntington in King Richard's time (the late twelfth century), and they do seem to have been associated with Barnsdale. On the minus side, it's the wrong Barnsdale (in Rutland rather than Yorkshire) and the earls of Huntington were actually Scottish royalty. There was a David, Earl of Huntingdon, who was the grandson of King David I of Scotland and took King Richard's side against his brother Prince John – but although he may have been the inspiration for Munday's plays, there is absolutely nothing to tie him to Robin Hood.

A number of people claimed to have seen an epitaph written on a stone in Kirklees, Robin Hood's traditional burial site, which confirmed the association with the Huntingtons.

There are many different versions, but the earliest recorded one reads:

Robert Earle of Huntington
Lies under this little stone
No archer was like him so good
His wildnesse named him Robbin
Hood
Full thirteen yeares, and something
more
These northern parts he vexed sore
Such out-lawes as he and his men
May England never know agen.

But there's no record of this epitaph existing at the grave until the seventeenth century – after Anthony Munday's plays. There's still an epitaph stone now at the grave thought to be Robin Hood's in Kirklees, but it reads a little differently, and is in pretty terrible, fake old-fashioned English – and the engraving doesn't look 700 years old.

The original writing on the gravestone seems to have simply said 'Here lie Robard Hude Wilm Gold burgh Thoms'. There's not much in that shared grave to denote a noble lineage, and even those few words have disappeared, thanks to the ravages of the weather and the curious hands of visitors.

In the eighteenth century, Dr William Stukely produced a family tree for Robin which made him Robert Fitzooth (this name apparently being 'easily corrupted' into Robin Hood), Earl of Huntington. No trace of the family Fitzooth has ever been found, nor anything to connect them to Huntington or Robin Hood. Back to square one.

What about Robin being Earl of Loxley instead? Loxley, at least, is in the right part of the country. It's now part of the Yorkshire city of Sheffield, not so far from Barnsdale and the other places associated with Robin Hood from the ballads. So how is Robin associated with Loxley? The first reference probably comes from about the sixteenth century (although the date of the manuscript is not certain) and has Robin being born in Loxley, while by the seventeenth century the antiquarian Roger Dodsworth has him being called Robin Loxley and born in Bradfield, Hallamshire – only a couple of miles from Loxley. (Dodsworth also has Little John being Earl of Huntley – why not share the nobility around?)

So Loxley joins the legend rather late, although it isn't an unlikely place for Robin to be born. But how does that make him noble? To answer that, you have to look at a minor noble called Robert Fitz Odo. Remove the 'Fitz' and you can see why he might be a candidate. And he was a lord of Loxley! And he owed money to the church! And he may even have been stripped of his knighthood and disinherited!

Case closed? Hardly. For a start, it was the wrong Loxley (in Warwickshire, this time) and there's no evidence at all that Robert Fitz Odo, whatever his financial problems, ever became an outlaw. In fact, there's nothing to connect him to the forest outlaw at all.

So Robin wasn't earl of Huntington, or of Loxley, or of anywhere else. The problem with ennobling him isn't just the difficulty in finding an aristocratic candidate who fits, it's in the fact that all the early accounts of Robin Hood have him being a non-noble doing non-noble things. He doesn't take an interest in politics or feudal factionalism, as you would expect. There are stories of Robin being reconciled to a king and having his crimes forgiven, but there's no suggestion of him ever getting an inheritance back.

And then there's the archery. Picture Robin Hood and you probably picture him with a bow and arrow. In the old tales, he's always associated with archery – which was a non-noble pursuit. If he had been of noble birth he should have learned to do the kind of martial arts you perform on horseback – fighting with swords, lances and maces, not the humble bow and arrow.

Maybe it's our innate snobbery that makes us want our heroes to be secretly aristocratic, or royal, or at least super-wealthy, but Robin was none of those things. He was just a commoner like the rest of us

3: He fought in the Crusades

It's a powerful image, a brave soldier returning from the hell of war in the Holy Land back to merry, green England, only to face another kind of war, this time against injustice and devious usurpers. This picture of Robin Hood is pretty closely tied to the idea of him as a nobleman, which we now know is bunkum, but ordinary people sometimes went on Crusade, too. Could Robin Hood have been one of them?

Well, there are a few problems with that, not least that the idea of Robin going on Crusade only pops up for the first time in 1849, in a novel by a chap called Joachim Stocqueler, whose life was as exotic as his name. In between several marriages and travelling around India, Afghanistan and the USA as a soldier and then a journalist, this Englishman found the time to write several books, including *Maid Marian, the Forest Queen*.

He seems to have lifted a lot of ideas for this novel from Sir Walter Scott's *Ivanhoe*, which features both a commoner called Robin Hood (or Locksley) and a knight called Wilfred of Ivanhoe who returns from the Crusades, remains loyal to King Richard despite ill-treatment by the evil Prince John, and whose fortunes are restored when Richard returns. Mix these two characters together and you produce an exciting story of Robin Hood the crusader – but you don't produce any reason for thinking that the medieval outlaw Robin Hood actually went on Crusade.

So could he just have been waiting faithfully at home the whole time for King Richard's return, as he does in some versions of the story? Well, that very much depends on when Robin Hood was around. And unfortunately for the Crusades/King Richard story, he probably wasn't born until long after Richard was dead.

When people think about 'the Crusades' in the context of Robin Hood and King Richard, they're thinking about the Third Crusade, in the 1190s. Nicknamed the Kings' Crusade, this is the one that Richard the Lionheart went on, along with Holy Roman Emperor Frederick Barbarossa and King Philip II of France. Richard took an inordinately long time coming back from the Crusade because he was kidnapped on the way home, although even this was doing better than poor old Frederick, who died on the way out.

Anyway, England was waiting with bated breath for the return of Richard, who finally turned up in 1194 after the payment of a painfully large ransom. To show his gratitude to his now impoverished kingdom, Richard stayed in England almost a month before shoving off to France for the rest of his life. All of which means that, in order to have been waiting around eagerly for Richard, Robin must have been haunting the forests of Yorkshire in 1194. Which he wasn't.

The earliest chroniclers who mention Robin Hood put him in 1283, 1266 and 1294-99. Don't let those very exact dates fool you; these men were writing chronicles, with events arranged by year, so they had to put him in somewhere specific, whether it was right or not. And where did they get their information about Robin Hood from? Almost certainly from the ballads of

Robin Hood that were sung up and down the country, which were likely to be much less concerned with exact dates than with Robin's derring-do. Even so, you would think that these three dates, all in the late thirteenth century, would put paid to the idea of Robin being around during the Third Crusade. Except that a century later, another chronicler, John Major, did put Robin Hood in the time of King Richard and Prince John.

Did John Major know something the other chroniclers didn't? Probably not. After all, he also had Robin Hood stealing from the rich to give to the poor, and leading a band of 100 archers, which indicates that it had all gone a bit fairy-tale by the time he was writing. But if that's not a good enough reason to ignore John Major's outlier date, there are other ways we can at least guess at the time Robin was plundering Barnsdale.

It's easy enough to find a date that Robin Hood must have lived before. The poem *The Vision of Piers Plowman*, which dates from about 1377, has a character called Sloth who claims:

> I know not perfectly my
> Paternoster [Lord's Prayer] as the
> priest it singeth,
> But I know rymes of Robyn Hood
> and Randolf Earl of Chester.

That means that whenever Robin was around, it was before 1377; and probably quite a bit before, if songs about his exploits were doing the rounds. But that doesn't help us when it comes to extricating him from the Crusades. For that, you have to look more closely at the details in the early ballads.

There are elements of the ballads that are typical of the thirteenth century. For example, Robin's encounter with a scary friar and his trained attack dogs (no jolly Friar Tuck, this one) couldn't have taken place in the twelfth century, because there weren't any friars. The mendicant orders (called friars from the French for brother, *frere*) were founded in the thirteenth century. The word 'yeoman' also isn't seen in English until about 1300, but the ballads are addressed to yeomen, and portray Robin as a yeoman.

And then there are technical details, like when Robin, in the *Gest of Robyn Hode*, asks Sir

Richard if he has been made a knight against his will. This system of forcing men with a certain level of wealth to become knights, and to pay a tidy sum to the Crown of the privilege, was called distraint of knighthood, and was introduced by Henry III, who (in case you're rusty on your regnal dates) reigned from 1216 to 1272. Edwards I and II used this money-making scheme too, but it mostly fell out of use after Edward III took the throne in 1327.

That would all be very neat, and place Robin Hood squarely in the thirteenth century, where the chroniclers said he belonged, if it weren't for the fourteenth-century details that are also in the ballads. There are technical details again, the kind of things that keep medieval historians in work. For instance, the corrupt sheriff in the *Gest* says he's paid a retainer by the nefarious abbot in the form of money and clothes. This was a particular problem in the early fourteenth century.

But then there's the overall mood and message of the whole legend, which fits nicely into the fourteenth century, a period of famine, plague, and huge inequality and oppression, culminating in the failed Peasants' Revolt of 1381. This is the sort of background where an outlawed commoner who outwits and overcomes the forces of law and order could become a popular hero, even a symbol of defiance.

Of course, that doesn't mean that Robin Hood necessarily lived in the fourteenth century, just that his story was popular then. The thing about oral tradition is that it's easy for bits to get added in that reflect the period when the story is being told, rather than the time it's set. But oral tradition does also preserve stuff from the time when the events actually happened, even if it sometimes ends up a bit garbled. So you would expect the earliest tales of Robin Hood to reflect the time they were told – the fourteenth century – and they do. But if these were stories about things that happened in the time of good King Richard and evil Prince John, there should be elements from the twelfth century too – and there's nothing. The monarch in the *Gest of Robyn Hode* is 'comely' King Edward, not good King Richard.

In this case, it seems the early chroniclers

were right. The Robin Hood the ballads were based upon must have lived in the late thirteenth or early fourteenth century. That does leave open the remote possibility that Robin could have gone on the ninth, and last, Crusade to the Holy Land in 1270, with Prince Edward (later Edward I) – but we'll leave that kind of wild invention to novelists like Joachim Stocqueler.

4: His enemies were King John, Guy of Gisborne and the Sheriff of Nottingham

King John was not a popular man. While he was Prince John, he was compared unfavourably with his absent but dashing brother, King Richard. Then during his own seventeen-year reign he managed to fall out with several members of his court, the clergy, the common people, the French, the Pope, and most of his own barons. As a result, he was forced to sign the Magna Carta, which took away some of his powers. He seems like the ideal candidate to be an enemy of Robin Hood – corrupt, power-hungry, hateful and lascivious. Except that we have already established (in chapter three) that Robin Hood was almost certainly born after John shuffled off this mortal coil in 1216. 'The king' hardly features in the early sources ballads at all, and when he does, he's a respected character, and he's called Edward.

What about Guy of Gisborne? Is he a more realistic enemy? Well, Guy is a bit of an oddity. You might be familiar with a sneaky, dangerous Guy of Gisborne, always neck-deep in plots and intrigue and much given to dark clothes and glaring. Or you might know him more as a buffoon, a comic foil for the Sheriff of Nottingham, more likely to catch a cold than to catch Robin Hood. But you're unlikely to recognise him as a hired killer dressed up in a horse costume. Yes, a full-length horse skin, complete with mane and tail, is what Sir Guy wears when he first appears in the ballad *Robin Hood and Guy of Gisborne*. Why? Impossible to say, but it's likely to be something carried over from the paganism-based May Games[*] (of which there will be much more in the next chapter). It's

---

[*] The pretend horses used in the May Games were called hobby horses, although they were more like what we would think of as pantomime horses. Strangely enough, the 'hobby' in hobby horse is thought to be derived from the name Robin – and so is Dobbin, the name we still jokingly use for horses today.

possible that Guy has his origins in the character of Guiot, a friend of Marian in the French *pastourelles* that made their way into the English May Games. But that's speculation.

What is true is that whenever he turns up in the ballads, things get very violent (you probably don't want to read about what Robin does to Guy while you're eating your breakfast), and the Sheriff of Nottingham is always behind it. There's no trace of Guy of Gisborne in history, but obviously someone as important as the sheriff of a major town must be pretty easy to trace. So how well does the Sheriff of Nottingham fit the bill as Robin's arch-enemy?

There's one problem that's immediately obvious: if Robin was in Yorkshire, why was the Sheriff of Nottingham after him? It's true that Robin is also mentioned going to Nottingham and poaching in Sherwood, but Barnsdale is far beyond a Nottingham official's jurisdiction. This isn't an insurmountable problem. There were a few sheriffs of Nottingham who also held power of various kinds in Yorkshire, and a few sheriffs of Yorkshire who held power in Nottingham-shire. There were even a few men who were both

Sheriff of Nottingham and Sheriff of Yorkshire in the thirteenth and early fourteenth centuries.

One of them was Sir Henry de Faucumberg, who was sheriff at various times between 1318 and 1330. He obviously had a role to play in catching notorious criminals, as he was charged with tracking down the gang leader Eustace de Folville. He might not have been very good at this role, however, as Eustace died at an advanced age of natural causes. Sir Henry was also probably corrupt, which fits with the picture of Robin's sheriff; Faucumberg was investigated for extortion and corruption more than once, but the charges never stuck.

Another likely character was Sir Robert Ingram. He was never Sheriff of Yorkshire, but he held a huge number of positions in the Nottinghamshire and Derbyshire area. Between 1306 and 1334 he was Sheriff of Nottingham, MP for Nottingham, Mayor of Nottingham, Knight of the Shire of Nottingham, Knight of the Shire of Derbyshire and Mayor of Derbyshire. He must have been a busy man, which is perhaps why he employed the Coterels, a violent criminal gang, to do his dirty work for him. He overlooked their little misdemeanours in return, making him a suitably corrupt figure.

There are other candidates, too, lots of them, especially if you're prepared to go further back in history. There's Reginald de Grey, who in the 1260s and 70s was Sheriff of Nottingham-shire, Derbyshire and Cheshire, and of the Royal Forests, as well as being constable of Nottingham Castle. Further back still there's Brian de Lisle and Eustace of Lowdham, both of whom held office in Nottinghamshire and Yorkshire in the early thirteenth century. But all this digging up of likely sheriffs for Robin Hood may be missing the point. The sheriff in the legends of Robin Hood is anonymous and vague. There's never any proper explanation of his vendetta against Robin Hood; he just serves as a symbol of The Law – and a very corrupt law at that.

A sheriff in the middle ages was the local representative of the authority of the crown. He had a financial role (very handy for extortion and misappropriation of public funds) and he administered the local legal system, including putting juries together (very handy for perverting the course of justice). It was a system wide open to corruption, as was the medieval legal system in general. Everything was stacked against the commoner, which was why some people chose to become outlaws rather than risk court. The tales of a famous outlaw are the perfect medium to air grievances about the corrupt and unreachable agents of the law – or in fact, of the Church; Robin's enemies in the ballads are just as likely to be bishops, abbots and archbishops as they are to be sheriffs. Church leaders held power as landowners, and could be just as corrupt and heartless as the forces of the law.

But none of that explains why Robin's enemy is always given the title 'Sheriff of Nottingham'. One theory is that there were tales and ballads about the Sheriff of Nottingham in his own right, maybe based on one of the high-profile sheriffs like Sir Robert Ingram, and it struck some balladeer as a good idea to combine them. According to this theory, the only reason the Robin of the ballads ever appears in Nottinghamshire is to allow the connection with the famous Sheriff of Nottingham – and it is true that the Sheriff of Nottingham appears in every single ballad that mentions the town of Nottingham. If their tales really did start off separate until they were combined later, like those of Batman and Superman, then it's pointless to look for a Sheriff of Nottingham who was in post when Robin was active, because they may not even have been alive at the same time. The Robin Hood who preyed on travellers through Barnsdale was certainly wanted by the law, but exactly who attempted to bring him to justice, we have no way of knowing.

5: His true love was Maid Marian

Everyone knows that Robin Hood's one true love was Maid Marian. In some versions of the story she is the servant of a noble lady; in other versions she is from the nobility herself; and in still others, just to confuse matters, she is one pretending to be the other. But whatever her social status, she loved Robin and he loved her, right? Well, no. In fact, they never even 'met' until centuries after Robin's death, and Marian didn't exist anyway.

Shortly after 1500 it was still possible for a character in a poem by Alexander Barclay to say he wanted to hear 'some mery fit [tale] of maide Marian or els of Robin Hood'. Stories of both Maid Marian and Robin Hood were obviously doing the rounds, but there was no connection between them. It wasn't until 1601 that they turned up together in a play by Anthony Munday, with 'Marian' being a pseudonym of

Matilda, daughter of Lord Fitzwater, Robin being the Earl of Huntingdon, and the whole thing being set in the time of King Richard and Prince John.

Elizabethan playwrights aren't known for their strict adherence to historical facts (check out the real history of Macbeth, if you want proof), and Anthony Munday was probably more casually ahistorical than most, but he didn't make Marian up from scratch, and he may not have been the first to introduce the two lovers to each other. So where on Earth did Marian come from?

The short answer seems to be: France. There was a series of French *pastourelles* (lyric poems and plays) featuring a shepherdess called Marion (as she was spelled in the French version), and usually her lover Robin too. This Robin had nothing to do with Robin Hood, and was usually a shepherd or a ploughman. Marion attempts, with mixed success, to fend off the lascivious intentions of a passing knight, and Robin sometimes helps. But the plot isn't really the point; the stories usually end with everyone celebrating with songs, dancing, feasting and general revelry, and this is how Marion found herself carried across the sea and incorporated into May Games.

There are still villages in England where May Day is celebrated with a Maypole and morris dancers, but in the late Middle Ages they took it very seriously, to the extent that you could be fined if you were elected May King or Queen and refused to play the role. Despite this all being a pagan fertility ritual, the church often put up the money to pay for the costumes, and then used the festivities as a fundraising event, not that different from a twentieth-century church fête, though probably with more drinking and fornication. In some locations by the early fifteenth century, 'Robin Hood' and his men pop up to collect the contributions (taking money off people was their forte, after all). By this point Robin was just a legendary figure to be incorporated into the fun, with no connection to the morris dancers or to Marion; he wasn't *her* Robin. But the passage of time has a tendency to mix things up and mash them together, especially when names are similar. By the late fifteenth century all the May Day characters were dancing merrily together with the morris men, and Marion the shepherdess had a Robin again, but this time it was Robin Hood.

So much for Maid Marian/Marion. But how did Munday dream up the idea of Robin's lover being the noble Matilda? The lady Matilda probably gets her name from a number of famous Mauds. (If you weren't confused enough already, the name Matilda is a variant of Maud.) There's Maud de Braose, a French noblewoman who lived in Wales. She fell out with King John, was pursued by him, and ended up being starved to death in captivity. Maud le Vavasour, who lived at around the same time, hailed from the north of England. She was married to Fulk FitzWarin, who also fell out with King John (John wasn't the most amenable type), was made an outlaw, and had to take to the woods, with Maud accompanying him. Finally, there's Maud Fitzwalter de Clare, whose name is almost as long as her claim to Robin Hood fame: her father fell out with King John (more proof of John's winning ways) and claimed that John had tried to seduce his daughter, but even if that's true, their quarrel had far more to do with power struggles between the barons and the king in the run-up to the signing of the Magna Carta.

Add that all together and you get a noble lady whose lover is an outlaw, who is persecuted and/or pursued by King John, and who spends at least some time hiding in the woods – our Maid Marian, in short. But Anthony Munday just made it all up from odds and ends of history, legend and poetry.

(By the way, there was a real-life Robin Hood in fourteenth-century Yorkshire who was married to a woman named Matilda, but given how common those names were, that's not terribly surprising. This Mr Hood seems to have been a law-abiding citizen.)

So was there no woman in Robin's life? There was no special romantic interest, I'm afraid, but there was one woman who was very special to the Robin of the ballads in a different way: the Virgin Mary. In the *Lyttell Geste of Robin Hood* he risks his life to travel to Nottingham and worship at her chapel, and the same piety crops up in other ballads too – usually towards the Virgin, sometimes towards another biblical Mary, Mary Magdalene. That's not to say that the historical Robin was necessarily a devout man; highway robbery is not encouraged in the Bible. It's more likely that this theme was added to the ballads to highlight the unchristian activities of the monks and abbots who appear, and to make Robin's attacks on them seem justified. A churchgoing audience might feel a qualm about applauding the exploits of a man who robbed from the church just for private gain, so better to make him a good Christian who deplores the corruption of the church (and the medieval church could be pretty corrupt).

Robin Hood's life, as far as we know, was a bachelor one, his time spent almost entirely with other men. But which men?

6: He had a band of merry men such as Friar Tuck and Alan a Dale

You can probably name the most prominent members of Robin Hood's gang. Little John – of course. Will Scarlett – check. Much the Miller's Son – sorry, who?

Poor old Much. Despite being one of only three merry men named in the early ballads, he has been mostly forgotten. Much does crop up in some modern versions of the legend, but usually as a very minor character. We don't know a lot about him, if 'know' is even the right word for a half-forgotten character from medieval poetry. 'Much' isn't a real name, so it must have been a nickname. Sometimes it's written as Midge instead, so he might have been short or not fully grown. In one ballad he carries Little John, which would suggest that he was strong, although you can hardly rely on little details that are useful to the plot. In another ballad, Much kills a child who witnessed a crime, so perhaps it's better that he's forgotten.

Other characters who remain in the Robin Hood legend, however, have a far weaker claim to his fame. Friar Tuck is one. He seems to be a combination of two characters, neither of whom had anything to do with Robin Hood originally. There's Robert Stafford, a real Sussex chaplain who became an outlaw and led a gang of murderers and robbers in the early fifteenth century. He called himself 'Frere Tuk', although whether he made the name up or he got it from somewhere else, we don't know. Either way, there's no obvious connection to Robin Hood.

Then there's the fat, jolly friar from the May Games. Maid Marian got her first introduction to Robin Hood through this relic of paganism, and the same plays and games that featured Marion (before she was Robin's girlfriend) also featured a jolly friar. He was more closely associated with Marion than Robin – perhaps very closely associated sometimes; this character fell into the tradition of the lecherous clergyman.

This combination of none-too-similar religious figures shows in the way Friar Tuck enters Robin Hood's tales. In his earliest appearance in the late fifteenth century, he's a tough, aggressive man, probably like Robert Stafford. There's an unnamed friar in a slightly later ballad who fights Robin and his men with a sword, shield and pack of fierce dogs. However, by the next surviving source a century later, Friar Tuck is strong and capable, but also a source of physical comedy and lewd jokes; Robin offers him a lady of loose morals to induce the randy friar to join the merry men. It's this earthy, buffoon character that stuck, as far as the legends are concerned, although he often retains some fighting skills, in a vague nod to the bandit who gave him his name.

Alan a Dale is a late addition as well. He appears in the seventeenth century as a young man whose intended bride has been taken away from him by a wealthy knight, but even this role was probably stolen from Will Scarlett in an earlier version of the story. Robin, of course, uses his cunning and trickery to help Alan get his bride back, on the condition that Alan join the gang. He sees them married (in some versions he impersonates a priest, so they may not strictly be married, but no one seems to care) and the newlyweds go back to the forest with Robin. Alan hangs around in later versions of the story, playing his lyre as a minstrel in Robin's service, but his happily married status doesn't really ring true; despite authors' insistence on adding a love interest to the legend, a violent band of wanted men, such as Robin's, was very much a bachelor society.

Among his bachelors, though, you will find some familiar names. Little John and Will Scarlett were not shoehorned into Robin Hood's story centuries later. In fact, Little John is not only closely associated with Robin Hood from the earliest ballads, he even finds his way into a historical reference to Robin Hood (in Andrew of Wyntoun's *Orygynale Chronicle*) and he may have been a real member of Robin Hood's gang. 'John le Litel' and 'Littel John' turn up in West Yorkshire court rolls in 1318 and 1323, charged with house-breaking, theft and poaching deer. John's grave is supposed to lie in the Derbyshire village of Hathersage, about 30 miles from Barnsdale. While there's no proof that the Hathersage grave actually belonged to the Little

John of legend, the bones that were exhumed from it in the eighteenth century would have belonged to an exceptionally tall man.

Will Scarlett, or Will Scathelocke, or a myriad other spellings, is also with Robin from the start, at least as far as the ballads are concerned. Attempts have been made to find the historical person behind him, but the results are less convincing than with Little John. There was a William Schakelock who in 1316 served in a garrison in Berwick, on the Scottish border, and a William Scarlet who was pardoned of felonies in 1318. If they were the same person (and that's a big if), it's vaguely possible that he could have been Robin's Will Scathelocke/Scarlett. But that probably wasn't Will's real name, anyway; Scathelocke means lock-smasher, or burglar.

So once you've removed the jolly friar (or chaplain-turned-bandit) and the romantic lyre player, you're left with a child-killer and two burglars, along with a few dozen others. (The ballads give Robin anywhere from about 20 followers to over a hundred.)

How kind of these cutthroats to devote themselves, and their ill-gotten riches, to the plight of the poor...

7: He robbed from the rich and gave to the poor

A'Robin Hood' is someone who takes from the rich to give to the poor. You can even label redistributive taxation 'Robin Hood politics' if you want. You can probably conjure up from your memory an image of Robin distributing coins from the coffers of greedy old abbots and grasping sheriffs to grateful common folks. But why did a medieval outlaw take it upon himself to support the suffering poor? He didn't, of course.

Robin takes plenty of money off the rich in the medieval ballads, but there are literally no incidences of him doing it for the benefit of the poor. Not that the Robin Hood of the ballads is selfish with money – he's quite happy to pay people over the odds for goods, to make loans, and to promise new suits of clothing to his followers. (This was before the industrial revolution; think Prada prices rather than Primark.) But giving to the poor? Nope. Taking from them was another matter. The jolly, loveable Robin Hood of the ballads might not actively hurt the poor, but he demands money with menaces from a potter, a butcher, a shepherd, even some pedlars – hardly the upper echelons of society.

In fact, the ballads almost certainly give Robin far too much credit. They are fictionalised accounts, after all, and the minstrels had to at least hint that there was something admirable in the wanted criminal they were singing about. Robin Hood is hardly unique here; you can find the same thing happening in the tales of other outlaws, ancient and modern.

There's a ballad from the same sort of period as the Robin Hood ones which tells the tale of outlaws Adam Bell, Clim of the Clough and William of Cloudesly. These three are frequently described as 'good yeomen', and the last stanza wishes 'God send them eternal bliss', even though the main distinction they seem to have achieved in the narrative is killing hundreds of people in Carlisle, many of them innocent bystanders.

Then there's Jesse James, most definitely a real person, who lived from 1847 to 1882. He seems to have been a fairly nasty piece of work. He and his brother Frank were implicated in all sorts of unpleasant deeds, from massacres of unarmed troops in the American Civil War, to bank and train robberies, to murder.

But that didn't stop someone composing a ballad of lament at Jesse's death, calling him a 'friend to the poor' who would 'never rob a mother or a child' nor 'see a man suffer pain'. Presumably that didn't include the cashier of the Gallatin bank, who probably suffered some pain when Jesse James shot him dead.

You can probably think of positive portrayals of other murderers and thieves too – John Dillinger, Billy the Kid, the Krays. The point is that a bandit doesn't actually have to be noble, kind or generous to be labelled a Robin Hood. Even Robin Hood wasn't a Robin Hood. It's just that in lawless times, when the weak can't count on the protection of the state, it's comforting to think that there are strong men who can stand up to their oppressors.

It's also fun to live out our own fantasies of disobedience through them, as long as they're not too bad. If these accidental heroes actually care about justice and freedom, great. If not, it's easy to reshape them in a more acceptable mould later, once they are dead and memories are fading. As a former college sportsman once said, 'the older I get, the better I was.'

So if Robin Hood was no Robin Hood, how bad was he? He was an outlaw – that's one of the few certain facts we know about him – but that didn't necessarily mean much by the thirteenth or fourteenth centuries. In earlier centuries an outlaw was someone who was so uncontrollably dangerous that he was removed from the protection of the law and could be killed by anyone with impunity – 'wanted dead or alive', essentially. But by the time Robin was around, you could be made an outlaw just for missing four county court sessions when summonsed. In fact, some people found being outlaws preferable to taking their chances with the harsh and corrupt medieval legal system. Sure, their land would be forfeit, but that wasn't much of a deterrent to those who didn't have a great deal to lose in the first place. 'Because of fear of prison, many an outlaw will be made,' says a fourteenth-century protest song.

Of course, the fact that you didn't have to be very bad to be an outlaw hardly proves that Robin was a nice chap. Highway robbery was rife in England in the late middle ages. Gangs of thugs roamed around, sometimes protected by gentry and clergy, sometimes even directly employed by them. These were harsher times, when mutilation was considered a fitting legal punishment, and the Robin of the early ballads is a man of his times – violent and dangerous, though trustworthy and loyal. That's the acceptable, fictionalised image; the historical chroniclers called him a murderer and a robber. Given his base of operations (on the high road through Barnsdale) and the kind of company he kept (burglars and thieves) it's more than likely that Robin Hood was just a successful highway robber who robbed everyone, rich and poor, to give to himself and his cronies.

So aside from the constant popular demand for heroes to stick it to the man, what could have resulted in a criminal like this getting a reputation for generosity to the poor? We probably have to go back to those May Games again. (Sorry.)

The idea first turns up in the sixteenth century, quite some time after the events were meant to have taken place, and in the meantime Robin Hood had become a stock character in May Games and festivals of that type. 'Robin' and his men, being thieves, were often used to collect contributions from the audience – contributions that went, via the church, to charitable causes. So 'Robin' was taking from the rich (well, everybody really) and giving to the poor (via the church).

Whether this was how the idea got started or not, by the early sixteenth century the chronicler John Major felt able to state that Robin only stole from the rich, and gave stolen ecclesiastical money to the poor. (Major also said that Robin only killed innocent people if they resisted being robbed, so that's comforting.) Writers in the seventeenth and eighteenth centuries picked the idea up and ran with it, along with Robin's aristocratic background, of course, and by the time Errol

Flynn donned the tights in the early twentieth century the idea was so entwined with the Robin Hood legend that it's the main thing people 'know' about him.

If you could go back in time and tell the real Robin Hood that, he'd probably laugh – then take your wallet and smartphone, and possibly shoot you.

8: He was called 'Robin Hood' because he wore a hood

'Robin – the hooded man.' These four words are the entire lyrics of the spooky Clannad theme song to *Robin of Sherwood*, the 1980s TV series. Not very elaborate, but surely accurate. After all, that must be what the 'Hood' in Robin Hood means, mustn't it?

Well, no, for a number of reasons. Hoods weren't particularly unusual attire in the Middle Ages. Calling someone 'Hood' to indicate who you meant would be about as useful as calling someone 'umbrella user' today. You may know that English surnames tend to fall into four broad categories: those based on location (e.g. Stirling), occupation (e.g. Taylor), heredity (e.g. Johnson) or a notable characteristic (e.g. Long). Hood could be a notable characteristic, except it's not that notable (unless it was a purple hood with yellow spots or something). It's far more likely Hood is an occupation-based surname. Someone called Hood would have made hoods.

The second problem is that Hood was a fairly common name, at least in Yorkshire, in the thirteenth and fourteenth centuries. In the early Middle Ages, surnames were more fluid than they are now, and a man's surname could alter as he moved about or changed profession. But they weren't entirely fluid, and the custom of passing them down generations was becoming established by Robin's time. Rather than Yorkshire being the centre of a thriving hood-making industry, it's likely that the preponderance of Hoods in medieval Yorkshire indicates that the name was being passed on. So a man called Hood might simply have been a descendent of someone who had made hoods.

But the third, and most complicated, reason, is that Robin Hood's name probably wasn't Robin Hood at all. In the fourteenth century robbers were nicknamed 'Robert's men' or 'Robert's knaves'. Robber, Robert – get it? And Robin is, of course, a diminutive of Robert. Now you could argue that this was inspired by Robin Hood himself, just as we use the description 'modern-day Robin Hood' ourselves. Or you could argue that it's simply coincidence; just because Robert sounds like robber, it doesn't mean you can't have a robber who is really called Robert (or Robin). But the problem is that the use of 'Robin Hood' to mean an outlaw seems, paradoxically, to date back to before the time of Robin Hood.

From the thirteenth century onwards, variations of 'Robin Hood' were used to denote outlaws. In a court roll from 1262, a fugitive called William had 'Robehod' added to his name. This was in Berkshire. That's far too early for the Yorkshire Robin Hood to have garnered such a huge reputation that his name would be a byword almost 200 miles to the south. But there was a much earlier bearer of the name, who did come from Yorkshire.

Between 1226 and 1234, a 'Robert Hood, fugitive' appears several times in Yorkshire court rolls. He is also called Hobbehod, and he appears to have owed money to the church. The Sheriff of Yorkshire is named as responsible for the sum owed, presumably unless he caught Hood and made him pay. Eventually his name disappears from the rolls, although whether because he paid up, or because he was prosecuted, we don't know.

If Hobbehod was the same man as Robert of Wetherby, 'outlaw and evildoer of our land', who was also pursued by the Sheriff of Yorkshire in the 1220s, then he came to a very sticky end; financial records of the pursuit of Wetherby end with a receipt for two shillings spent on a chain to hang his body.

So was this the 'real' Robin Hood? Probably not. All right, he owed money, and that was an offence, but it's hardly the kind of notorious crime that gets ballads composed about you. If Hobbehod and Robert of Wetherby were the same person, then he was a more serious criminal threat, and a lot of money was spent on his capture, but we don't *know* that they were the same person – just that they were both called Robert and both got into trouble with the law in Yorkshire in the 1220s. Either way, there's no apparent connection with a criminal band, and he/they had nothing to do with Barnsdale (or indeed Sherwood), the location of Robin Hood's famous exploits. It's not impossible that this obscure figure is the inspiration behind the legend, but a more realistic possibility is that a robber *nicknamed* Robin Hood, who did lead a gang in Barnsdale, and who was a dab hand with a bow and arrow, became inseparably associated with the name. Maybe Hobbehod, fugitive from justice, was the source of the nickname. Maybe not. But wherever it sprang from, a successful Yorkshire robber made it his own, like a chart-topping cover version that obscures the very existence of the original.

But if the 'Hood' in Robin Hood has nothing to do with his headgear, what did he wear? That's a difficult question to answer. The classic image of Robin Hood, with his three-pointed, feathered cap and neat green tunic with dagged edges, comes from Victorian times. There are no contemporary images of Robin Hood at all. By the time many of the surviving Robin Hood ballads were printed, in the seventeenth century, the illustrated woodcut characters look ready to step into a Stuart court. There are occasional references in the ballads, however, which suggest that Robin and his men wore Lincoln green.

Now at this point someone is bound to bring up the point about Lincoln green actually being Lincoln *graine*, a top-quality scarlet cloth. There are numerous nineteenth- and twentieth-century images of Robin wearing red, presumably based on this idea; but the idea is almost certainly wrong. First, scarlet is rather a conspicuous colour for a wanted man to wear, particularly a yeoman. Peasants usually wore dull colours created from natural dyes, or even greyish undyed cloth. Red was for the nobility.

Of course, Robin could have ignored this social convention just as he ignored the law, but the second reason why he probably didn't wear red Lincoln graine is that, as often as not, his clothes are simply described as 'green', not 'Lincoln green'. The villagers who played Robin Hood and his merry men in the May games were definitely clothed in green, not red. In fact, it had become a sort of shorthand for identifying the forest outlaws, much as it is now; if you see a man on his way to a fancy-dress party dressed in a green tunic and tights, you know who he's going as.

Lincoln graine can perhaps be found in the

Lyttell Geste of Robyn Hode, where it's described as 'scarlet and grene' (possibly a mistake for 'scarlet in graine'). But here Robin, who seems to be moonlighting as a draper in this ballad, provides the cloth to a knight – just the sort of person who might be expected to wear red. When Robin recruits a new man to his gang in The Jolly Pinder of Wakefield, however, he offers him as a sweetener two outfits a year, one in Lincoln green and one in brown – nice, dull colours that will blend in, both to the countryside and to society. None of this proves that Robin actually wore green. It might be a detail that was added on later during the May festivities. He may have worn mud brown, or oatmeal, or that perennial medieval favourite, washed-out blue. But he almost certainly didn't wear red.

And on his head? Robin Hood may well have worn a hood, whether an ugly linen coif tied under the chin, or a generous chaperone that fell over his shoulders, or a hood with one of those unfathomable rat's tail adornments (called liripipes) down the back. Or he might have worn a hat. Or perhaps he went bareheaded. But whatever he wore, he did not get his name from his headgear.

9 He was really…

Every few years there seems to be a story in the papers about how someone has identified the 'real' Robin Hood, and then it is forgotten again until someone else discovers a completely different 'real' Robin.

There are quite a few candidates for being the original Robin, or at least the inspiration for the story. Some of the obscure ones have already been mentioned in earlier chapters, but other candidates are famous and important enough to deserve being sent packing individually. So, ladies and gentlemen, allow me to introduce to you five pretenders to Robin Hood's longbow.

...Fulk FitzWarin

You may remember Fulk from chapter five. His wife, Maud le Vavasour, was probably one of the models for the noble Lady Marian, which might provide a link to Robin Hood if the Lady Marian hadn't just been made up by an imaginative playwright, and if non-noble Marian had any-thing to do with Robin Hood in the first place. Leaving that aside, what reasons are there for thinking that Fulk FitzWarin could be our man?

Fulk (or Fouke, or however you prefer to spell it – this was before standardised spelling) was a baron in the Welsh Marches, probably born in the 1170s. The story of his life was trying to get, and keep, Wittington Castle, on the Welsh border, as well as various other properties. King John had a tendency to sign them away to other nobles, who were very happy to take them, leaving Fulk trying to get them back by legal or illegal means. He became an outlaw during this dispute, and had to live in the Welsh Marches with his followers while he tried to defeat the schemes of the evil King John. Now you can see the resemblance, can't you?

There was also a romance written about Fulk in which he used disguises and tricks to outwit his enemies, much like the Robin Hood of the ballads. But if you've been paying attention at all, you'll probably already have spotted some flaws with the idea that Fulk FitzWarin was either the real Robin Hood, or the inspiration for him.

For a start, both time and place are wrong. The romance of *Fouke le Fitz Waryn* is set mainly between 1200 and 1203, the period of his first fight against King John. (They were reconciled, but fell out again later during the Barons' War, when John refused to put the reforms of the Magna Carta into practice.) This is almost certainly too early for Robin Hood.

The action takes place in Wales and the southwest of England, places that have no connection with Robin Hood whatsoever. And then there's the fact that all of Fulk's motivation has to do with his wealth and status as a noble. He rebels against the king in defence of his ancestral lands and to increase the power of the English barons. Robin doesn't have any land, and there's no indication that he ever did. He's a commoner who spends his time with other commoners. When he's reconciled to the King in one of the stories in the *Gest of Robyn Hode*, he's offered employment, not his land back, let alone a strategically important castle.

For:

>>—▶ Lived in the wild with a band of followers

>>—▶ Used cunning and trickery against his enemies

>>—▶ Good with weapons

>>—▶ Was reconciled to the King (like Robin in the *Gest*)

Against:

>>—▶ Wrong time

>>—▶ Wrong place

>>—▶ Wrong social class

>>—▶ Mainly interested in getting his castle back

…Hereward the Wake

Our second candidate is Hereward the Wake. He was an Anglo-Saxon resistance leader against the Norman invasion. Hereward had been a landowner from an important family in pre-Norman times, but the invasion of 1066 changed that. He returned from a period abroad to find that his ancestral lands had been taken away. Hereward set himself up on the defensible Isle of Ely in Cambridgeshire with a band of similarly angry and dispossessed men, and started a guerrilla war against William the Conqueror and his French invaders. Hereward was important enough to make it into both the Doomsday Book and the *Anglo Saxon Chronicle*, as well as having his own very imaginative and unreliable romance, *De Gestis Herewardi Saxonis* (The Deeds of Hereward the Saxon). In 1070 he burned and sacked Peterborough Abbey, and the following year he was driven off the island and had to take refuge in the Northamptonshire fens and forests. He may have been reconciled with the king later, but it's not certain.

Initially it's not at all clear why anyone would connect Hereward the Wake and Robin Hood. Hereward was around so much earlier that he was practically living a different world, pre-Norman England, speaking Anglo-Saxon and waging war against foreign invaders, not robbing passing tradesmen. But there are curious similarities in the stories that were told about them, and not just general things about tricks and disguises. In *De Gestis*, Hereward happens to meets a potter, persuades him to swap clothes and lend him his wares, and uses this disguise to get close to his enemy, William the Conqueror. In *Robin Hood and the Potter*, an early ballad, Robin Hood does exactly the same thing, but in order to trick and then trap *his* enemy, the Sheriff of Nottingham.

Surely it can't be a coincidence? Probably not. But does it mean that Robin is in fact secretly based on Hereward? Again, probably not. Have you heard the story about the library that is slowly sinking because when they designed the building, they forgot to account for the weight of the books? So have I – but I've heard it applied to a few different libraries. Good stories tend to get borrowed and reused, and to survive even when their original context has disappeared. It means that the story about an outlaw swapping clothes with a potter was around long before Robin Hood was born, so his legend borrowed it from Hereward's (who could have borrowed it from somewhere else). It doesn't mean that Robin Hood was based on Hereward the Wake, any more than the French Resistance in *'Allo 'Allo* was, cunning ruses notwithstanding. Despite what Sir Walter Scott might have thought, Robin was not a high-minded Saxon resistance fighter, he was just a medieval English robber.

For:

➤ Lived in the wild with a band of followers

➤ Used cunning and trickery against his enemies

➤ Good with weapons

➤ May have been reconciled to the King (like Robin in the *Gest*)

Against:

- ⟫⟶ Wrong time
- ⟫⟶ Wrong place
- ⟫⟶ Wrong social class
- ⟫⟶ Mainly interested in resisting the Normans and getting his land back

…Eustace the Monk

Contestant number three is Eustace the Monk, who deserves to be better known in his own right. There aren't many people whose career trajectory takes them from monk to court official to pirate, with accusations of witchcraft thrown in along the way. Eustace was born about the same time as Fulk FitzWarin, the 1170s, but in France. He was the son of a Boulogne noble, Baudoin Busket. After an education in Spain (allegedly specialising in black magic), Eustace took up religious orders, but soon left them in order to try to avenge the death of his father. He was not successful, so instead he entered the service of the Count of Boulogne, Renaud of Dammartin. So far, so *Princess Bride*, but it's what happened when he fell out with Renaud that links him to Robin Hood: Eustace was accused of financial mismanagement, his properties were confiscated, and he took to the forest.

This was a very short episode in Eustace's life – probably only a year or so – but an enterprising biographer wrote an account of his exploits that made a lot of this year in the forest, full of cunning ruses and imaginative revenge borrowed from other story traditions. The story of dressing up as a potter finds itself into this romance, as well as Hereward's and Robin's.

Arguably it's the part of Eustace's life after this little forest escapade that is more interesting. He had previously fought for the French King Philip Augustus, trying to reclaim territories from King John. After his falling out with Renaud, the Count of Boulogne, Eustace set up for himself as a pirate in the English Channel, then entered the service of King John, fighting against Philip Augustus. When John and Renaud made a treaty of friendship, Eustace switched sides back to King Philip Augustus, supplied arms to the northern barons rebelling against King John, and carried the French Prince Louis over to England to try and capture territory. Eustace and his miniature navy eventually made the Channel unsafe to cross for anyone not on his side (whichever side he happened to be on at the time), and established the island of Sark as his private kingdom. Eustace was eventually defeated and captured by English forces in the

Battle of Sandwich, and beheaded on the spot.

Fascinating though Eustace's life was, there's not much resemblance to Robin Hood apart from that one year, around 1203 to 1204, when he hid out in the forest. He was a French nobleman whose career was almost entirely naval. A few overlapping stories of tricks and disguises aren't enough to get around a difficulty like that.

For:

>>→ Lived (briefly) in the wild with a band of followers

>>→ Used cunning and trickery against his enemies

Against:

>>→ Wrong time

>>→ Wrong country

>>→ Wrong social class

>>→ Spent most of his career at sea

...William of Cassingham

Also known as Willikin of the Weald, William of Colingeham and half a dozen other things, William's origins are obscure but his career was brilliant. While Eustace was helping the French to take over large parts of southern England, William was defending it with a large band of local archers. William's men harassed the French forces in a guerrilla war, and then when things started going England's way (after the death of the hated King John in 1216), they ambushed Louis' forces, pursued the survivors and cut off their supplies. The French nearly died of starvation before their fleet arrived. When Louis later tried to return to Dover, he found that William had destroyed the French camp there, and had to land elsewhere.

William might be forgotten these days, but he was recognised at the time. He was given land, position and an income for life, while his wife was taken under the king's protection after William died in 1257. 'Weald' means forest, and Willikin of the Weald's forest-based guerrilla warfare with bows and arrows might suggest

Robin Hood, if it weren't for the fact that he was active exclusively on the south coast of England; he fought for King John against the French; and he was, as far as we know, never an outlaw.

For:

- Fought in the forest with a band of followers
- Archery

Against:

- Wrong time
- Wrong place
- Never an outlaw
- Mainly interested in defeating the French invasion

...Roger Godberd

Last, and most convincing, is Roger Godberd. He actually has a lot going for his claim to be the 'real' Robin Hood. He was an outlaw in Nottinghamshire in the late thirteenth century, and the Sheriff of Nottingham was charged with capturing him. Roger was even accused of poaching deer in Sherwood Forest (or, less excitingly, Charnwood Forest), and of robbing an abbey and killing a monk, rather like Robin in the ballads, although this outrage was in Wiltshire rather than Yorkshire.

Roger and his gang were accused of crimes in Nottinghamshire, Leicestershire, Derbyshire and Wiltshire. While none of these is Yorkshire, a Yorkshire knight called Richard Foliot was accused of harbouring Roger and his accomplices. Sir Richard's castle at Fenwick was only about five miles from Barnsdale, Robin's base of operations. The Sheriff of Yorkshire was sent to take Fenwick Castle on account of Sir Richard sheltering Roger – which is very reminiscent of the Sheriff of Nottingham being sent to take Sir Richard at the Lee's castle in the

Gest of Robyn Hode, because he was sheltering Robin. Roger was even pardoned by the King at one point (King Henry III in this case), although he continued with his criminal career afterwards.

So is there anything against this northern outlaw being Robin Hood? Unfortunately, there are a few things. Walter Bower, a chronicler who mentions Roger Godberd and his crimes, also mentions Robin Hood and puts them in roughly the same context, as men who became outlaws during the fall-out from Simon De Montfort's rebellion against Henry III – but he treats them as two separate men. Roger Godberd was often associated with another outlaw, Walter Devyas, and some people have speculated that this must be Little John, but there's literally nothing linking Walter Devyas and Little John apart from the desire for Roger to be Robin Hood. The names aren't similar, and there's no record of Walter ever being nicknamed John, or Roger being nicknamed Robin, or Hood.

There are also a few things in Roger's life that don't really tie in with what little we know about Robin. The Sheriff of Nottingham who pursued him, Reginald de Grey, had been a pal of his. Roger was on the garrison of Nottingham Castle before he became an outlaw, and he and Reginald had merrily poached deer together in 1264. Then there's the fact that Roger kept getting caught. There are certainly legends where Robin Hood is caught, briefly, and broken out by his men, but Roger spent a long time in Newgate Prison after being captured in 1272, and was probably executed there. He also had no connection to archery, as far as we know, and there are no tales of him using disguise or trickery.

Despite all that, though, it's only fair to admit that some of the parallels are strong – so strong that Roger's escapades probably influenced the Robin Hood legend.

For:

- Right place (roughly)
- Right time (possibly)
- Outlaw and bandit with a band of followers

Against:

>»—▶ No archery, trickery or living in the wild

>»—▶ Arrested and possibly executed for his crimes

The main problem with all of the men listed here, however, is that they were real people with real names, dates, and historical records, and none of them is ever associated at all with the nickname 'Robin Hood'. Their legends certainly influenced Robin's; in the case of Roger Godberd, who was from roughly the same part of the country, bits of his real story may even have drifted into the Robin Hood legend. But if we want to find a real Yorkshire outlaw who went by the name of Robin Hood, we're not going to find him here.

10 So what do we know, then?

If you could go back in time to discover where the truth behind the Robin Hood legend lies, what would you find? First of all, you'd have to decide when to set the controls of your time machine for. I think 1320 would be a good bet, although you might have to jump around a bit between 1250 and 1350 before you found what you were looking for. Where to travel to is easier: Barnsdale, in Yorkshire. You could park your machine beside the bridge in Wentbridge and head up the steep hill out of the village. If you paused for breath (as you probably would) and looked up towards the Sayles above you, you might see distant figures moving in the trees, but you probably wouldn't. However, from their vantage point high above the village, a band of outlaws would have seen you the moment you stepped off the bridge, and if you looked worth robbing, they would be waiting for you.

And just who would be waiting for you? It's unlikely it would be a band of 100 accomplished archers, but it wouldn't be surprising if there were a few arrows trained on you. After all, it was a common enough weapon, and especially handy for ambush. The men carrying these bows (and knives, and axes) would be commoners, and would probably look much like any peasants you saw as you passed through the village, although perhaps their clothes would blend in a bit better with the greenery, and they might look a little better fed.

You wouldn't be able to understand their language, in all probability, but if you had invested a bit of time studying Chaucer in preparation, and if they were willing to talk, what would you discover about them? The leader might call himself 'Robin Hood', but he might not; that nickname might have been applied to him later, by the minstrels who composed the ballads. He would certainly have had a real name, if he cared to tell you it. You might see a very tall chap called John, towering over a rag-bag of assorted villains and ne'er-do-wells. If you got them talking, the stories of how they ended up in a criminal gang would range from accounts of corrupt authority figures abusing their power, to hard luck tales of failed harvests and family illness, to plain greed, vice, and the kind of things we euphemistically call 'poor life choices' these days.

And if they invited you to join their gang (which probably happened less frequently in real life than it does in ballads), what would you spend your time doing? Robbing other travellers coming up the difficult hill out of Wentbridge, where horse-powered transport could manage no more than a slow walk. You would especially look out for government officials or other important people travelling from York to London, hopefully carrying a lot of money, preferably without too big an armed guard for you to tackle. The rest of your time you would spend dodging the authorities and spending your illicit wealth until someone informed on you, or an armed guard proved too much for you, and you met an unpleasant end.

But here's the thing: you might come across a very similar situation whether you put your time machine down in 1280 or in 1320, or somewhere in between. It's possible that the legend of Robin Hood, the bow-slinging archer, was based on more than one Yorkshire highwayman. Highway robbery was a constant problem, and similar bands of ne'er-do-wells probably waited on top of Sayles, or other handy spots of the Great North Road, at lots of different times during the thirteenth and fourteenth centuries. One of them probably had a lieutenant called Little John. One of them would have been very good with a bow. One of them might have had a thing about fighting anyone he invited to join his band, one on one. They wouldn't necessarily all have been the same person. Over time the tales told about them would have merged, along with the most memorable stories from other outlaws such as Hereward the Wake and Roger Godberd, until they produced Robin Hood, the audacious archer we find in the earliest ballads, leading his band of men in a violent but carefree outlaw life. You can strip away all the companions added by the sixteenth-century May Games, and the nobility (of birth and character) added by seventeenth- and eighteenth-century playwrights, and the pretty clothes and crusading history welded on in the nineteenth century. If you do, you get back to one or more outlaw archers leading a bunch of highwaymen who infested Barnsdale in the late thirteenth or early fourteenth century. But to be any more accurate than that, you really would need a time machine.

Further Reading

Bellamy, J (1985) *Robin Hood: An Historical Enquiry,*

Bradbury, J (2010) *Robin Hood*

Carpenter, D A (2004) 'Eustace the Monk (c.1170–1217)' in *Oxford Dictionary of National Biography*

Dobson, B and Taylor, J (1989) *The Rymes of Robin Hood: An Introduction to the English Outlaw*

Evans, M R (2005) 'Robin Hood in the Landscape: Place-Name Evidence and Mythology' in H Phillips (ed) *Robin Hood: Medieval and Post-Medieval*

Holt, J C (1989) *Robin Hood* (2nd edition)

Holt, J C (2004) 'Hood, Robin' in *Oxford Dictionary of National Biography*, Oxford University Press

Howlett, S (2007) 'Barnsdale' in R Ovens and S Sleath, (eds) (2007) *The Heritage of Rutland Water*

Keen, M (1961) *The Outlaws of Medieval Legend*

Knight, S (ed) (1999) *Robin Hood: An Anthology of Scholarship and Criticism*

Knight, S (1994) *Robin Hood: A Complete Study of the English Outlaw*

Knight, S (2006) 'Robin Hood and the Crusades' in *Florilegium* 23.1, 201-22

Lowe, B. (1955) 'Robin Hood in the Light of History' in *Journal of the English Folk Dance and Song Society*, 7(4)

Ohlgren, T H (ed) (2005*) Medieval Outlaws: Twelve Tales in Modern English Translation* (revised edition)

Phillips, H (ed) (2005) *Robin Hood: Medieval and Post-Medieval*

Pollard, A. J. (2004) *Imagining Robin Hood: The Late Medieval Stories in Historical Context*

Stephens, G (1941) 'A Note on William of Cassingham' in *Speculum* 16(2)

Waltz, R B (2013) *The Gest of Robyn Hode: A Critical and Textual Commentary*

Online resources

The Robin Hood Project: University of Rochester: http://d.lib.rochester.edu/robin-hood

Robin Hood, Bold Outlaw of Barnsdale and Sherwood: http://www.boldoutlaw.com

Robin Hood Legend: http://www.robinhoodlegend.com

Acknowledgments

I am grateful, as ever, to Dayspring Jubilee Macleod, my excellent editor, to my sister, Lynne Bradey, for an incredibly speedy beta read, and to my mother for her constant encouragement.

I am also grateful for the patience of all the friends, family members and acquaintances whose ears I talked off about this project. Thank you for your forbearance!

About the Author

K C Murdarasi is a Scottish author based in Glasgow. She studied Ancient History at the University of St Andrews, where she also took modules in Medieval History, Philosophy, Ancient Greek and other impractical subjects. She is as astonished as anyone else to find that she still uses her degree on a regular basis.

You can find out more about the author on her website: kcmurdarasi.com. Or follow her on Twitter: @kcmurdarasi.

You can order further copies of this book direct from Hephaestion Press, with **free** UK delivery.

To order, email Hephaestion.Press@gmail.com or visit hephaestionpress.wordpress.com